To the
patient 😊

in /2018.

The art of being ill

The art of being ill

JILL SINCLAIR

FREIGHT BOOKS

First published 2014

Freight Books
49-53 Virginia Street
Glasgow, G1 1TS
www.freightbooks.co.uk

A CIP catalogue reference for this book is available from the British Library

ISBN 978-1-908754-83-7
eISBN 978-1-908754-84-4

Printed and bound by Hussar Books, Poland

To my Mum for all her expert
and kind mopping of my brow.
And for my demented Dad whose brow
I've been soothing, for being such
an exemplary patient.

How to use this book
Disclaimer – this book is not intended for someone
critically ill or in need of urgent medical attention.
If in doubt please consult a health professional.

CONTENTS

FOREWORD
by Dr. Sarah Jarvis

I haven't quite been a GP long enough to remember the days when the doctor's word was law, but sometimes it feels like it. These days, everyone has access to apparently limitless information at the touch of a button – and as every doctor will attest, that's not always a good thing. With the internet almost entirely unpoliced, I have grown used to patients presenting with questions about coffee enemas and 'miracle' cures, with cyberchondria and scare stories that make it harder for them to trust me.

But being empowered brings so many benefits, too. **Patient.co.uk** has seen its traffic rise to an astonishing 16 million views every month, with people accessing accurate, peer reviewed information written by GPs for GPs and their patients. People want information, and they want to know how to look after themselves. This book, by turns lighthearted and practical but always pragmatic and sound, is a great addition to any potential patient's reading list – and that includes all of us. It debunks myths, tells you why sometimes mother really did know best, and carries you through the journey from that first sniffle to full recovery. Hurrah for the art of being ill.

Dr Sarah Jarvis, GP and clinical consultant to **Patient.co.uk**

INTRODUCTION

I was a sickly child. Being at war with my tonsils from an early age meant I was used to being ill. It's not as easy as it seems. Mastering the art of resting and recovering takes time and a certain skill. Not everyone has the knack. So this book is for those people who have never been ill, or who are illness novices and need a bit of guidance.

It will also come in handy if you are recovering from a broken bone – that takes real talent and, until it's happened to you, you will not know the delights and difficulties of getting around on crutches, making a cup of tea with your arm in a sling or keeping your plaster cast dry in the bath.

My uncle – a doctor – used to say, 'There are no Brownie points for being brave when you are really ill.' Better to get on and be brilliant at it.

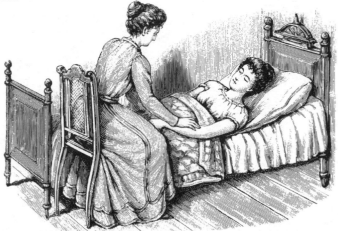

There is one consolation in being sick; and that
is the possibility that you may recover to a better
state than you were ever in before.

Henry David Thoreau

HOW TO GET ILL

I'm sorry that you're ill!

It's wretched. No-one likes to be ill. It can feel like you've failed in some way. What have you done to deserve it?

Did you go out with wet hair? (if you did, don't beat yourself up, it isn't the cause of your cold.)

Did you forget to wash your hands? (in which case you have only yourself, and the person before you who left the germs that you picked up because they also forgot to wash their hands, to blame.)

Did someone sneeze over you? Eugh! (see facts on sneezes.)

And how exactly did this illness make its way to you?

Infections can be caused by both **bacteria** and by **viruses.** They have a number of ways of getting into your system:

- By one person breathing in another person's infected cough or sneeze.
- By eating infected food.
- Via an open wound or a bite.
- Through sexual contact.
- The faecal–oral route, when poor hygiene means that faecal matter* gets on hands or food and is then ingested.
- You could be infected by insects or ticks, which can carry the likes of Yellow Fever and Dengue Fever (although not in the UK as far as we know).
- Finally, you could be infected by warts and by syringes that haven't been properly sterilised.

* (faecal is the medical term for poo, shit, crap, poop, doo-doo, jobbie – or whatever else you might call the stuff that comes out of your bottom)

VIRUS vs BACTERIA

Both bacteria and viruses can cause infections and the only way to be sure which you have is by testing. Your doctor might take a throat swab or a sample of spit.

The crucial difference between a virus and a bacterial infection is that antibiotics (also known as anti-bacterials) don't help in the treatment of viruses.

And if you take antibiotics unnecessarily you are storing up trouble for later when your body has got used to them, so they aren't as effective.

Bacterial infections include Tuberculosis, Pneumonia, Cholera, Typhoid, Tetanus, Diphtheria, Bacterial Meningitis, Gonorrhoea, Syphilis, Scarlet Fever, Strep Throat, Bacterial digestive infections.

Viral infections include Colds, Flu, Glandular Fever, Chicken pox, Measles, Mumps, Herpes Simplex, Herpes Zoster (also known as Shingles), Yellow Fever, Hepatitis A & B, Viral Gastroenteritis, AIDS, Rabies, Polio.

Many illnesses nowadays can be avoided altogether by vaccinations.

SUPERBUG BACTERIA

DETAILED 3D ILLUSTRATION OF A VIRUS
INFECTING THE HUMAN BODY

————————— Deadliest Diseases of All Time —————————

This Top 10 chart changes as some illnesses are eradicated and others emerge. There was a time before we had AIDS and when you'd be more likely to die from Bubonic Plague than Cancer.

In 2014 there was a new candidate for the chart – although it may not make it into the Top 10 of All Time. **The Ebola virus.** With a fatality rate of 90%, it so far occurs primarily in remote villages in Central and West Africa, near tropical rainforests. It's thought that Fruit bats are the natural host of the Ebola virus. So far there is no specific treatment or vaccine available for use in people or animals. Scary!

Here are some of the deadliest diseases of all time

1	AIDS	6	Tuberculosis
2	Cancer	7	Diabetes
3	Malaria	8	Smallpox
4	Tetanus	9	Whooping Cough
5	Cholera	10	Measles

Let's hope you are suffering from something a little less dramatic than Smallpox or Cholera. A cold perhaps, or flu. Even an 'itis': tonsillitis, laryngitis, pharyngitis, tracheitis. Or maybe an unspecified bug which is laying you low.

Many of the symptoms of these everyday illnesses are similar – headache, temperature, swollen glands, general feelings of being unwell. That's your body's way of telling you it's fighting an infection and you need to take notice.

∞∞∞∞∞ BE PREPARED ∞∞∞∞∞

Assuming that you've taken all necessary precautions to avoid being ill *(see Keeping Well)* and despite your best efforts you are, in fact, poorly, you will have a much easier time of it if you are prepared.

So now what happens?
Any illness, however you come by it, is an invasion by something unpleasant and unwanted that your body has to fight off.

In order to get better, your body has to put on its armour, gather up its arsenal of recovery tricks and get into fight mode. It can be a messy business. And it can use up a lot of energy.

What happens next?
A bit like those African porcupines that empty their bowels at the first hint of danger so that they are lighter and can run faster, one of the first signs of illness might be diarrhoea.

Other bodily fluids – like sweat and mucus – are also intended to flush out the invading illness and accompanying fever.

It is usually better to let your body get rid of this stuff than to hold on to it. Taking medicines to stop you having diarrhoea or to stop your nose running might only be delaying the inevitable. If you can, it's a good idea to let your body do what it needs to. And make yourself comfortable for the ride.

Much of what you need when you are indisposed will already be in your house: face flannel or tea towel, hot water bottle, sick bucket or bowl, aspirin and loo paper.

STORE CUPBOARD ESSENTIALS

A well-stocked store cupboard ought to also include the following:

Utensils

Large jug or bottle for water

Bucket or bowl for being sick into. (If you have to use the washing up bowl or a fruit bowl be sure to disinfect it properly once you are fully recovered and before it goes back into service.)

Loo paper or wet wipes (wet wipes can't be flushed down the loo but there is a new breed of wipes which can – best to have these handy for both ends, if you think they'll end up down the loo.)

Thermometer no longer the ones made with mercury that you could so easily press against a hot water bottle or radiator to get a really high reading, modern day thermometers are digital and are stuck in your ear, under your arm or under your tongue to get a reading.

·· Food and Drink ··

Water – water is the single most important aid to recovery. It flushes out infection and toxins, it rehydrates vital organs so that they can function properly and it helps to reduce your temperature and keep you cool. Water from the tap is usually fine but if you've had a bout of food poisoning or gastroenteritis – anything where vomiting has been involved – it's wise to drink water that's been boiled and allowed to cool down.

Honey – can be soothing in a drink or to eat, has antiseptic properties and is a source of energy.

Coca Cola, Pepsi, Ginger Ale, Lucozade, Sprite and Lemonade – can all help with rehydration after sickness and/or diarrhoea. Drink these if you don't have access to water and/or you need a bit of sugar to perk you up. DO let it to go flat and/or dilute with water to reduce its gassiness. DON'T only drink as an alternative to water. Have water as well wherever possible.

Coconut water – contains essential electrolytes, is sugar and fat free, another great source of hydration.

Tins of fruit – mandarin segments, peaches, fruit salad. And fresh bananas, oranges, grapes, melons where possible. Fruit is a good source of fluid, vitamins and sugars.

Lemon – also useful in a drink to combat the symptoms of colds and flu, helps reduce catarrh and is a source of vitamin C. Easily available in bottles or those squeezy lemon shaped dispensers. Use fresh where possible.

Vinegar (see *In Praise of Vinegar*)

Soup – you can freeze cartons or tubs of soup or keep a couple of emergency cans.

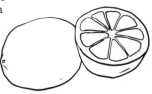

Medication

(see *The Drugs Do Work*)

Aspirin – for pain relief.

Paracetamol – for pain relief and to reduce temperature.

Ibuprofen – for pain relief.

Dioralyte – for rehydration.

Vaseline – for soothing chapped skin.

Vicks Vapour Rub – to reduce congestion in a blocked nose.

Hand sanitiser gel – a good alternative to soap and water, although never as good as washing with soap and water.

Vitamin C – helps to aid recovery.

Echinacea (according to the *Lancet Infectious Diseases*, taking Echinacea cuts the duration of the symptoms of a cold).

Over the counter cold treatments such as Lemsip or Beechams Powders*.

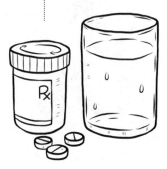

*Take care to read the ingredients of any medication in case it includes Paracetamol. It is important to avoid taking two lots of Paracetamol by mistake – the consequences can be fatal.

It may help to keep a chart of the medication you've taken so that you don't exceed the maximum doses.

Be sure to keep all medicines out of the way of small children.

Comforters

Hot water bottle – useful if you are cold, have pulled a muscle or period pains.

Ice pack or cold flannel – to reduce temperature or swelling.

A box of soft tissues – especially if your nose is raw from blowing.

Bed Socks – if your feet are cold, you will feel cold.

Spare pyjamas – in case of accidents or spillages, or just to make you feel fresher and less smelly.

Favourite cardigan or bed jacket – to keep you warm and to cover you up in case of unexpected visitors.

Radio/music/TV – for company and so you can keep track of the time.

Phone – to make those all-important calls to your Recovery Team and, in extreme situations, to the medics.

Cuddly toy – optional.

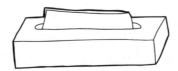

Probably best not to have your pets too close while you're ill. Keep them at arm's length until you are at the convalescence stage. (Although obviously don't forget to feed them, or arrange for someone else to.)

While we're at it, might as well mention the First Aid Kit.

According to St John Ambulance we should all have the following in our first aid kits:

First Aid Kit

Assorted waterproof plasters – used to cover minor wounds.

2 medium sterile dressing pads – used to cover severe wounds.

2 large sterile dressing pads – bigger version of above, used to cover severe wounds (bigger than needs a plaster).

4 triangular bandages – used to support broken limbs and make slings.

2 pairs of sterile gloves – used to prevent infection being passed on.

Good quality tweezers – for removing splinters.

Something for alleviating the symptoms of a sting – such as antihistamine cream/spray.

Savlon or other antiseptic cream – not to be used on open wounds, can be used on minor skin irritations and infections such as spots.

1 crepe bandage – can be used to hold dressings or ice packs in place, should not be used as a support bandage.

2 sterile eyepads – to cover wounds to the eye, they are just a dressing cut to the shape of the eye.

1 pair of paramedic scissors – used to cut clothing if needed.

Alcohol-free wipes – used to clean hands and around minor wounds.

6 safety pins – used to tidy up ends on slings.

Tape – used to tape down dressings if needed.

Many First Aid kits can be bought ready-made from chemists. For more information and in case you want to become a qualified first aider, contact: St John Ambulance **www.sja.org.uk** Or the Red Cross **www.redcross.org.uk**

If you have a run-of-the-mill cold there's no real need to know your temperature, but if you think you might have something more sinister it's worth keeping any eye on it.

Normal body temperature is **37C** or **98.6F**. If your temperature is over **38C** or **100.4F** then you have a fever (high temperature).

Your temperature will vary according to the time of day (lower in the morning than during the day or in the evening), the ambient temperature in the room, at different times during the menstrual cycle, and before and after eating.

These are the average daytime temperatures for an adult.

Measurement Location	Average Temperature	Fever Temperature
Ear	37.6°C (99.6°F)	38.0°C (100.4°F)
Mouth	36.8°C (98.2°F)	37.5°C (99.5°F)
Armpit	36.4°C (97.6°F)	37.2°C (99.0°F)

Do follow the instructions and only use a thermometer as intended.

∞∞∞∞∞∞ COLD OR FLU? ∞∞∞∞∞∞

Colds and flu have a lot in common.

Symptom	Cold	Flu
Sneezing	✓	x
Cough	With mucus	Dry and can be acute
Sore throat	Often the first sign of a cold	Sometimes present with Flu
Runny nose	✓	x
Blocked nose	✓	x
Feeling shivery	x	✓
Fever	Not so much	✓
Aching muscles	x	✓
Headache	x	✓✓
Feeling really weak and exhausted	✓	✓✓

Cold Control
Sneezes can travel at around 100 miles an hour
and are made up of between 40,000 and 100,000
droplets. So every unguarded sneeze carries
with it the potential to infect roughly the
entire population of a small town.

Cheers!

Having a cold may not pole-axe you completely but you will want to be rid of it as soon as possible.

Although strictly speaking there is no scientific proof that dairy products – milk, cheese, butter, yoghurt – encourage the production of mucus, they can make the bronchial tubes and sinuses 'sticky' so that it's harder to clear away the phlegm, so where possible avoid or reduce your intake of dairy foods.

Steam Vapours can help with unblocking your nose and making breathing easier:

Fill a shallow bowl with hot water, add a teaspoon of Vicks Vapour Rub, put a towel over your head and lean over the bowl. Breathe deeply through your nose if you can so that the steam is inhaled. A couple of minutes should make a difference and leave you with a clear nose. Do this a couple of times a day and especially last thing at night before you go to sleep.

Vicks is also useful if your nose becomes sore and cracked. Smear a small amount on the affected areas. Honey is also a good as a balm for sore and cracked skin. As is Vaseline.

Drinking hot honey and lemon has recognised health benefits. Honey has antiseptic properties, can ease soreness and reduce coughing; lemon is rich in vitamin C and helps to reduce mucus production.

The art of being sick is not the same
as the art of getting well.

Tony Snow

BUILDING A SICK BED
a beginner's guide

In the acute phase of your illness you need to stay in bed to give your body the best chance of recovery.

Try to move around as little as possible. But because you will need to be drinking plenty of fluids, you will have to get up to go to the loo. (Unless you are able to successfully pee into a bucket, and assuming you don't have diarrhoea.)

Building the perfect sick-bed involves having everything you need within easy reach. Along with a supply of water, you will need some or all of the Necessary Utensils and Comforters, plus food if you can face it.

☞**DO** also keep your phone handy, along with a charger so that it doesn't go flat.

☞**DON'T** forget to take any medicines that are specifically prescribed for your particular illness.

However ill you are, sooner or later you will get a bit bored so you will need some entertainment. A book, radio, TV, computer. But don't spend precious recovery time getting in touch with your friends to tell them how poorly you are. Unless they are part of your Recovery Team (see *Making the Most of Your Family and Friends*).

Your sick-bed – especially if it's your actual bed – may become a bit smelly. A combination of sweat, wind, snot, saliva, spillages and general detritus, so it's a good idea to have a spare pair of pyjamas handy so that you can have a change of clothes and feel a little less grubby. Your visitors will also appreciate this.

The truly organised sick-bed architect will have two flannels – one for soothing their brow and the other for cleaning, with a bowl of water for washing. You don't need much water, just enough to give yourself a quick once over.

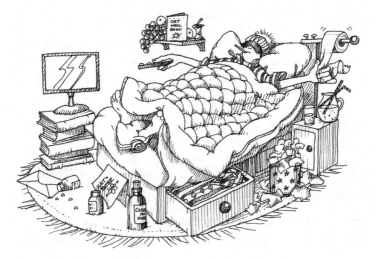

If you are new to building a sick-bed, a small bottle of handsanitizer is a good place to start. Use it to keep your hands clean, but don't use it as a face wash.

A toothbrush and toothpaste is useful if you have been sick, otherwise a mouthwash will probably be enough to take away the taste and any associated bad breath. Another thing your visitors will appreciate, although they ought not to be getting that close in the early stages of an illness. They're no use to you if they get ill too.

Loo paper is essential for mopping up, although can be a bit rough for nose blowing, so a box of tissues is another important piece of kit.

You may be alternately hot and cold, so you need extra blankets, socks, and a hot water bottle, as well as a way to cool yourself down. An ice pack on your forehead is the most effective way to bring down a temperature, but a wet flannel is a good alternative. It will feel cold at first but will then dry out or heat up and be less effective. Use cold water to wet the flannel and keep turning it over so that it feels cold.

Now you're properly ready to be ill.

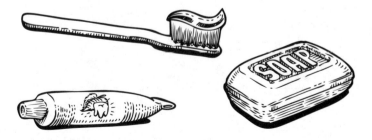

While we are asleep the body's immune system has the best chance of fighting infection and repairing damaged tissue.

AIDS TO RECOVERY

The best things you can do to speed up recovery are:

- Rest
- Drink plenty of fluids
- Stay warm
- Eat sensibly
- Take any necessary medication

Although staying in bed is important at the start of any illness, it isn't something you want to do for longer than necessary. Being in bed all the time is not good for your circulation, digestion or breathing.

Once out of the Acute Phase of your illness you can start getting out of bed and moving around. Although if you've been in bed for several days or even weeks you will feel a bit feeble. Don't overdo it or you risk having a relapse.

THE IMPORTANCE OF WATER

Water makes up approximately 70% of the human body. It is vital for digestion, keeping your joints moving, healthy skin and removing waste products.

If you feel lightheaded, dizzy and wobbly, and if your urine is very dark, you are probably dehydrated and need to drink something.

Water, diluted juices and herbal teas are all good sources of fluids. Caffeinated tea, coffee and fizzy drinks will make you need to go to the loo more often. Not ideal if you are still in the Bed Phase.

—————— 10 Reasons to Drink Water ——————

1. Water helps maintain healthy body weight by increasing metabolism and regulating appetite.

2. Water leads to increased energy levels. The most common cause of daytime fatigue is actually mild dehydration.

3. Drinking adequate amounts of water can decrease the risk of certain types of cancers, including colon cancer, bladder cancer, and breast cancer.

4. For a majority of sufferers, drinking water can significantly reduce joint and/or back pain.

5. Water leads to overall greater health by flushing out wastes and bacteria that can cause disease.

6. Water can prevent and alleviate headaches.

7. Water naturally moisturises skin and ensures proper cellular formation underneath layers of skin to give it a healthy, glowing appearance.

8. Water aids in the digestion process and prevents constipation.

9. Water is the primary mode of transportation for all nutrients in the body and is essential for proper circulation.

10. Water helps to reduce the symptoms of a hangover.

Water Facts

- A person can live for about a month without food, but only about a week without water.

- While the daily recommended amount of water is eight glasses per day, not all of this water must be consumed in liquid form. About 20% of our fluid intake comes from food.

- Soft drinks, coffee and tea, while made up almost entirely of water, also contain caffeine. Caffeine can act as a mild diuretic, preventing water from travelling to necessary locations in the body. So have these types of drinks in moderation.

- By the time a person feels thirsty, their body has lost over 1 percent of its total water amount.

- A word of caution – drinking too much water too quickly can lead to water intoxication. Water intoxication occurs when water dilutes the sodium level in the bloodstream and causes an imbalance of water in the brain.

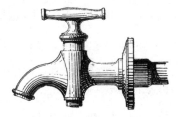

A glass of warm water with a slice of fresh lemon in the morning helps kickstart the digestion process for the day.

Lemons contain citric acid, calcium, magnesium, vitamin C, bioflavonoids, pectin, and limonene – all useful for promoting immunity and fighting infection. Lemons are antibacterial, antiviral, and lemon juice is a digestive aid and liver cleanser.

Almost certainly better for you than that double espresso or urn of tea! Especially while you are recuperating.

THE DRUGS DO WORK

Colds and flu can't be cured by over-the-counter treatments, but the symptoms can be alleviated.

Most cold 'cures' are made up of something to bring your temperature down, some pain relief, something to perk you up, a bit of vitamin C, something to dry up a runny nose and a decongestant. The powders that have to be diluted in hot water also make you drink, which is itself a vitally important part of getting better.

—————————— Cough Control ——————————

For a dry cough buy a **cough suppressant**.

Expectorants help bring up phlegm, so buy an expectorant if you have a chesty, loose cough.

Decongestants relieve the symptoms of cold and flu by reducing inflammation. Decongestants are not advised for people with high blood pressure.

················· Painkillers ·················

Painkillers – have slightly different uses. These are the ones you can buy over the counter – anything stronger will have to be prescribed.

Aspirin* one of the NSAID (non-steroidal, anti-inflammatory drugs)	Use for headaches, migraines, sore throat, toothache, neuralgia, arthritis, acute strain or sprain, muscle and joint pain, period pain, cold and flu symptoms.
Ibuprofen (another NSAID)	Use for fever, pain, period pain and inflammatory diseases such as osteoarthritis and rheumatoid arthritis.
NSAIDs are also available as a cream, gel or lotion rubbed into a specific part of the body.	For muscle pain, sprains and strains.
Paracetamol	Use for everyday aches and pains – headache, toothache, joint pains and to help reduce temperature.
Codeine**	Good for pain after surgery, broken bones, injuries and severe toothache.
Antihistamines are not painkillers as such but helpful nevertheless.	For some allergies, hayfever, insect bites and stings.

* Avoid taking aspirin on an empty stomach and never exceed the recommended doses of any drugs.

** Codeine can cause constipation. Be sure to drink even more fluids than usual and try to eat plenty of fresh fruit to avoid getting bunged up.

Aspirin

The active ingredient in aspirin, acetyl salicylic acid,
is the synthetic derivative of a compound, salicin, which
occurs naturally in plants, notably the willow tree.
Extracts of willow were traditionally used in folk
medicine and as early as 400 BC the Greek physician
Hippocrates recommended a brew made from
willow leaves to treat labour pains.

The Aspirin Foundation

Antibiotics can be broad spectrum, or specifically aimed at a particular illness. Some antibiotics kill bacteria, while others only prevent bacteria multiplying.

Antibiotics give some people diarrhoea. Ask your doctor about PRO-biotics to restore the good bacteria in the gut and help prevent upset stomachs. Live yoghurt is restorative and soothing (but it has to be the 'live' sort). Or try some of the pro-biotic drinks in the supermarkets.

Another possible side effect of antibiotics is **Thrush**, a fungal infection that can occur in your mouth or genitals. This might clear up of its own accord with time and a healthy diet, or may need a helping hand. You can buy treatments over the counter – having first asked for the advice of your pharmacist – or get a prescription from your GP.

——————— A Word of Warning About Antibiotics ———————

Antibiotic resistance is a serious and growing phenomenon in contemporary medicine and has emerged as one of the pre-eminent public health concerns of the 21st century.

A World Health Organisation report released in April 2014 says 'this serious threat is no longer a prediction for the future, it is happening right now in every region of the world and has the potential to affect anyone, of any age, in any country. Antibiotic resistance – when bacteria change so antibiotics no longer work in people who need them to treat infections – is now a major threat to public health.'

By taking antibiotics unnecessarily or by starting a course of antibiotics and not finishing it we are creating strains of superbugs that will be resistant to the antibiotics we have, leaving us at risk from all manner of illnesses and making some surgery too risky to attempt if the antibiotics won't work to combat infection.

HOT VERSUS COLD

Everyone is different. For some people warmth works, and for others it doesn't. But there are a number of general rules about when to apply heat and when to opt for cold.

For colds and flu where your temperature fluctuates you may need a hot water bottle and a cold flannel to soothe your brow when you're overheating.

A source of warmth can be very good for toothache and period pains and if you've got an achy muscle. However, there is a protocol for the early stages of an injury which cautions against warmth and advises the following:

72 hours after a sprain or muscle strain
- Avoid hot baths, saunas and heat packs

- Don't drink alcohol because it can increase swelling and delay healing

- Instead, in the case of an injury, adopt the P.R.I.C.E Procedure.

———————————— The 'Price' Procedure for Injuries ————————————

These are five simple steps that anyone can use to minimise the effects of immediate injury. Use the PRICE regime as soon as possible after an injury, the earlier the better. Take these five steps while waiting to be seen by the Emergency Services or before being treated by a Physiotherapist or other health professional.

P is for Protection ◦ Protect yourself and any injury from further damage. Keep the weight off a knee or ankle injury.

R is for Rest ◦ Allow an injury time to heal. Being brave is not always wise. Even a small injury needs time to recover.

I is for Ice ◦ By applying Ice onto the injury – an ice pack or even a pack of frozen peas – you will reduce the pain and inflammation. Always wrap ice in a cloth rather than apply directly to skin.

C is for Compression ◦ Compression of the swollen area will help to reduce the swelling. Using an elastic bandage, rather than a firm plastic bandage, is best. The fit should be snug enough to provide support, but still allow expansion for when muscles contract and fill with blood. Keep a close eye on extremities in case the bandage is stopping the blood flow and loosen or remove the bandage if you start to feel numbness.

E is for Elevation ◦ Elevating the injury to above the heart reduces the flow of blood to the area and reduces the swelling.

There are no Brownie points for
being brave if you are really ill.

Dr. Stanley Miller

————————— Your Recovery Team —————————

how to make best use of your family and friends

However much your friends like you, they will probably fall into two camps; those who want to help and those who will want nothing to do with you until you are fully recovered. In other words the Useful and the Useless.

How much you can ask for help also rather depends on the type of illness.

The days of measles parties are long gone. In fact measles has more or less been eradicated, but there was a time when Mums would invite other children to come round and play with their highly infectious offspring. Kissing was encouraged in the hope that these visiting children would go home the proud incubators of Measles (regular and German), Mumps and Chickenpox. These illnesses are better to have as children than as adults so if you could catch it, and get it over and done with before you hit puberty it was considered a blessing.

A childhood rite of passage.
With Ribena and cakes thrown in!

Nowadays vaccinations are available for all sorts of illnesses which mean that children are unlikely to have to go to measles parties; another reason why some people reach adulthood hopelessly unaccustomed to the art of being ill.

Assuming you aren't wildly infectious, and your friends include some of the Useful ones, you can put together your Recovery Team, and give the all-important answer to the question 'Can I do anything to help?' with a clear 'Yes, you can!' And then produce a list.

Even if you are supremely well organised it is advisable to accept help so that a) your friends can fulfil their mission to be Useful and b) because there will always be something that you need.

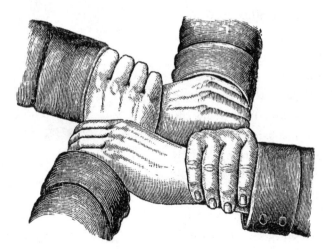

Convalescence looks good enough to the outsider.
A lazy life with people waiting on you hand and
foot, and nothing to do but eat and sleep.

In spite of this convalescents are known to bite the
hands that feed them... it is not really their fault.
For they are going through an awkward transition period.

The Convalescents' Handbook, Sheila Pim (1943)

☞**DO** say yes to more loo paper, softer tissues, some food you've developed a craving for. Fresh fruit, if you only have tinned. A prescription that needs collecting. A newspaper or magazine. A bottle of Lucozade. Check the list of store cupboard essentials and find something to ask for.

☞**DON'T** ask your friends to empty your sick bucket or makeshift commode. If you ask them to do something too gross you risk turning them from the Useful to the Entirely Absent.

☞**DO** share anything edible that your friends have brought. Remember, if it's a random gift they have most likely chosen it because they also like grapes, chocolate, peanuts, or whatever it is.

☞**DON'T** show your visitors anything that has come out of your body, from any orifice; any spots or rashes and anything you've picked out of a crevice through boredom.

☞**DO** ask those friends who can cook to do some batch cooking for you. Ask them to portion the food up and put it into Tupperware boxes so that you can fill your fridge with individual servings. Soups are ideal (see *The Truth About Chicken Soup*), so then you need only ask your next visitor to bring fresh bread to go with the soup (although bread can be frozen too). Fresh fruit smoothies are a good way of getting liquids and nutrients. Ask your Recovery Team to find a juicer and make up the drinks for you.

☞**DON'T** be embarrassed about asking for ice cream and jelly if you can't face anything else. If you can add a handful of fresh fruit, all the better.

☞**DO** show your Recovery Team your appreciation and say how much better you feel for their visit. Say that you'd be delighted to do the same for them! Ask them to call back in a day or so, leaving room for your other friends to visit so that you share out the workload.

SCHEDULING VISITORS

It's no good having all your visitors come at once – they will only end up talking to one another. And on other days you'll have no visitors at all.

☞**DO** schedule the times your visitors come to see you. If you generally feel better in the afternoons don't agree to a visit by someone on their way to college or work at 8 o'clock in the morning, especially if they are the cheerful types.

☞**DON'T** allow visitors to stay all day. Limit the time they stay to a maximum of 30 minutes in the acute phase of your illness. It can be longer as you start to recover and in the Convalescence Phase they can stay for long enough to cook you a meal or watch a movie (see *Convalescing in Style*).

Healthy Hint

Have your front door key on a piece of string that
you can lower out of the window so you don't have to
leave your bed to answer the front door. Not advisable
if you live on anything above the second floor.

MAKING MATTERS WORSE

If you want to prolong your illness (and why would you?) here's what to do.

- Soldier on regardless.

- Dose yourself up with cold cures, grab a packet of tissues and sneeze your way into college or work.

- Eat rubbish food.

- Only drink coffee or highly caffeinated soft drinks.

- Don't sleep.

If you follow this advice you could soon turn a simple cold into a more complex illness – bronchitis perhaps, or even pneumonia.

Don't think your friends and work colleagues will think you are clever for going into work and infecting them too. No-one likes being ill unless they are hypochondriacs – but even they may only *think* they're ill and really have nothing wrong with them at all.

Ideally aim for somewhere between reckless and hypochondriac when it comes to managing your health.

Famous Hypochondriacs

Adolf Hitler

★

Florence Nightingale

★

Andy Warhol

★

Charles Darwin

★

Hans Christian Andersen

★

Marcel Proust

★

Tennessee Williams

★

Howard Hughes

BITES & STINGS

Not all ailments are illnesses. Sometimes a simple, unprovoked and unexpected encounter with a small insect can leave you feeling sore and miserable.

A midge or mosquito bite won't kill you (in the UK) but can be very irritating.

The trick is to avoid being bitten in the first place.

Natural repellents, applied to the skin, include:

- Lemon
- Citronella oil
- White tea tree
- Witch hazel
- Lavender

You can also try altering your body odour and the 'taste' of your blood by taking:

- Garlic tablets for about a week before any possible encounters.

- Yeast tablets, or drinking beer.

- Vitamin B1 tablets or Marmite.

- Or try not washing or using shampoo – although this may end up being more unpleasant than the odd bite.

Environmental deterrents include:

◦ Mosquito coils – hung on a tree at a safe distance from camp. The smoke will deter most flying bugs.

◦ Citronella candles.

◦ Bug zappers – battery-powered lights that attract bugs and then kill them.

Physical barriers:

◦ Mosquito nets, inner tents with mesh, face nets and, thanks to the miracles of modern technology, you can now also buy clothing impregnated with insect repellent.

◦ In more extreme conditions you might want a chemical-based insect repellent, although there can be side effects and some may cause skin irritation and stinging eyes.

New products are coming onto the market all the time, so ask for advice in your chemist and specialist outdoor camping or clothing shops.

You are unlikely to avoid being bitten altogether, so be prepared.

In a midge swarm there can be around 40 thousand midges landing on your skin at any time.

Minimise the pain by using a clicker device to help neutralise the pain of bites. Apply creams, take antihistamines to quickly calm the itchiness.

Stings can be slightly more hazardous.

My friend Emily once unwittingly ate a bee sting which had somehow found its way into her lunch. Her face began to swell, her lips ballooned and her tongue doubled in size. Luckily she was engaged to a medical student at the time. He told us to take Emily straight to hospital. They admitted her immediately and gave her an injection to stop the swelling and prevent full-blown anaphylactic shock.

Assuming you are not allergic and having a life-threatening reaction to a sting, and that you have been stung by a solitary attacker rather than by a whole swarm, a sting is likely to be more annoying than serious.

Bees and wasps may look similar from a distance – and that is the best place to see them from – but they are quite different. Not least if they sting you.

Most people will have only a mild reaction to a sting and the pain usually lessens over a few hours. For some people the pain will last up to a week.

Don't give in to the itch and start scratching. You will only make the sting worse and may end up with an infection.

Bees are acidic, so the antidote to the effects of a sting by a Bee is something alkaline. Assuming you don't have a tube of something specific from the chemist, use an onion, cut in half and put the cut side over the puncture. Or use Baking Powder or Bicarbonate of Soda, mixed with a little water to create a paste and smooth it on the wound.

BUFF-TAILED BUMBLEBEE
(BOMBUS TERRESTRIS)

19TH CENTURY ENGRAVING
OF A POLLEN WASP

Wasps are alkaline so use acidic vinegar or lemon juice to neutralise the sting.

In both cases apply lavender oil or witch-hazel to the skin to reduce itching once the initial sting has been dealt with.

Healthy Hint!

Only bees leave their stinger in the skin.
If it is still there DO NOT try to pull it out
with tweezers, since this might have the effect
of squeezing more of the poison into the skin.
Try scraping out the sting with a clean finger
nail or something flat like the back of a
blunt knife or a credit card.

———————————The Trouble with Ticks ———————————

There is a tick borne disease – **Lyme disease** – which used to be rare but thanks to damper summers is becoming more common in the UK. A tick bite can be harmless – not all ticks carry the bacteria which produces Lyme Disease – but can also be very harmful.

The first and typical symptom of Lyme Disease is usually a rash that spreads out from the site of the bite. Left untreated, the bacteria can spread to other areas of the body. In some cases this can cause serious symptoms – often months after the initial tick bite.

After a human has been bitten by a tick, it usually takes 24-48 hours for the bacteria in the tick to pass into the human. **If you are able to remove the tick within 24 hours you are much less likely to develop Lyme disease, even if it was an infected tick.**

Beware: ticks are very small, and often do not hurt when they bite so it's quite easy to have a tick bite without noticing.

Erythema migrans rash
In the UK, most people with Lyme Disease get the 'bullseye' rash – a single circular red mark that spreads outwards over several days. The circle gets bigger and bigger with the centre of the circle being where the tick bite occurred.

The rash is not usually painful or particularly itchy. Without treatment, 'erythema migrans' typically fades within 3-4 weeks. However, just because the rash fades does not necessarily mean the infection has cleared from the body.

Symptoms of Lyme Disease can include **flu-like symptoms** – tiredness, general aches and pains, headache, fever, chills and neck stiffness.

The treatment for Lyme Disease is a course of antibiotics and ought to be started as soon after the bite as possible.

How to prevent Lyme Disease

- When out in the countryside – particularly where deer are present – keep to paths and away from long grass or overgrown vegetation, as ticks crawl up long grass in their search for a feed.

- Wear long-sleeved shirts and long trousers tucked into socks. Light-coloured fabrics are useful – it's easier to see ticks against a light background.

- Use a tick repellent on your skin, such as one that contains DEET.

- Inspect your body – including scalp, head and neck – each day to check for ticks and remove any that are on the skin.

- Shower or bath after returning from a tick-infested area.

- Check that ticks are not brought home on clothes.

- Check that pets do not bring ticks into the home on their fur.

How to remove a tick

- Gently grip the tick as close to the point of attachment to the skin as possible. Do this preferably using fine-toothed tweezers or forceps, or a tick removal device.

- Twist anti-clockwise and pull steadily upwards, away from the skin. Take care not to crush the tick.

Cheap tick removal devices may be available at veterinary surgeries and pet shops, and are useful for people who are frequently exposed to ticks. Always follow manufacturers' instructions.

DO NOT do any of the following:

☞**DO NOT** burn the tick off (for example, using lighted cigarette ends or match heads).

☞**DO NOT** apply petroleum jelly, alcohol, nail varnish remover, or other substances (as this may stimulate the tick to regurgitate potentially infected material into the skin, which may increase the risk of transmission of infection).

☞**DO NOT** use your fingers to pull the tick off.

☞**DO NOT** squeeze the tick.

After removal, ☞**DO** clean the skin with soap and water, or skin disinfectant, and wash hands.

For more information visit **www.patient.co.uk**

NATURAL KILLERS

The natural world is fraught with danger. But ought we to be more afraid of a lion than a dog? Or an elephant than a fly?

According to the World Health Organisation here are the number of people killed per year by each of the following:

Shark ⋯⋯⋯⋯⋯⋯⋯⋯⋯⋯⋯⋯⋯⋯⋯⋯⋯⋯⋯ 10
Wolf ⋯⋯⋯⋯⋯⋯⋯⋯⋯⋯⋯⋯⋯⋯⋯⋯⋯⋯⋯ 10
Lion ⋯⋯⋯⋯⋯⋯⋯⋯⋯⋯⋯⋯⋯⋯⋯⋯⋯⋯⋯ 100
Elephant ⋯⋯⋯⋯⋯⋯⋯⋯⋯⋯⋯⋯⋯⋯⋯⋯ 100
Hippopotamus ⋯⋯⋯⋯⋯⋯⋯⋯⋯⋯⋯ 500
Crocodile ⋯⋯⋯⋯⋯⋯⋯⋯⋯⋯⋯⋯⋯⋯ 1,000
Tapeworm ⋯⋯⋯⋯⋯⋯⋯⋯⋯⋯⋯⋯⋯ 2,000
Ascaris roundworm ⋯⋯⋯⋯⋯⋯⋯ 2,500
Tsetse fly (sleeping sickness) ⋯⋯⋯ 10,000
Assassin bug (Chagas disease) ⋯⋯ 10,000
Freshwater snail (schistosomiasis) ⋯ 10,000
Dog (rabies) ⋯⋯⋯⋯⋯⋯⋯⋯⋯⋯⋯ 25,000
Snake ⋯⋯⋯⋯⋯⋯⋯⋯⋯⋯⋯⋯⋯⋯ 50,000
Man ⋯⋯⋯⋯⋯⋯⋯⋯⋯⋯⋯⋯⋯⋯ 475,000
Mosquito (malaria) ⋯⋯⋯⋯⋯⋯ 725,000

─────────── In Praise of Vinegar ───────────

The types and uses of vinegar seem endless. Vinegar contains vitamins, minerals, amino acids, and can protect against heart disease and cancer.

∘ **Apple Cider Vinegar** – The healthiest of all vinegars, Apple Cider Vinegar, contains pectin, potassium, beta-carotene enzymes, amino acids, calcium, iron, magnesium and helps the stomach produce hydrochloric acid, which aids digestion. Phew!

∘ **Red Wine Vinegar** – Red Wine Vinegar is full of anti-ageing antioxidants, is cholesterol free, sodium free, and fat free.

∘ **Balsamic Vinegar** – High in antioxidants and potassium, Balsamic Vinegar was used as a gargle, tonic and air purifier against the plague. This is the vinegar that some people put on strawberries and over ice cream.

∘ **Thyme Vinegar** – Thyme Vinegar contains iron, magnesium, silicon and thiamine, can act as an antiseptic and general healing tonic.

∘ **Oregano Vinegar** – Oregano Vinegar is both antiseptic and anti-inflammatory. It kills bacteria, viruses and can help fight colds and flu.

∘ **Sage Vinegar** – A natural astringent and antiseptic, Sage Vinegar is recommended for the gum disease gingivitis and sore throats.

∘ **Rosemary Vinegar** – Rosemary Vinegar contains extra calcium, magnesium and potassium and may help to lower blood pressure.

———————————— Uses of Vinegar ————————————

1. On burns – firstly cool the burn under cold, running water, or use a cold flannel – do this as soon as you possibly can. Once you have cooled the burn as much as you can apply Apple Cider Vinegar directly on to burn to minimise inflammations and swelling. Apple Cider Vinegar also helps to relieve stinging and prevent blisters.

2. For sunburn, add a cup of Apple Cider Vinegar to your bath, and soak for 10 minutes to reduce discomfort.

3. Alleviate Athlete's Foot by rinsing feet with vinegar. The acid content of the vinegar helps stop fungus growth and relieves itching. The same applies to fungal toenail infections.

4. As an inhaler to relieve congestion – put a few drops of Apple Cider Vinegar in a bowl or mug of hot water and inhale the vapour.

5. Gargle with warm water and vinegar to soothe a sore throat.

6. On acne and cold sores – as an antiseptic and to dry out the spots.

7. Adding vinegar to the final rinse when you wash your hair can help eradicate dandruff and kill off head lice and nits.

8. Vinegar can be helpful when you have a headache – put a dab on a damp cloth, put the cloth on your forehead and lie down.

9. For indigestion and heartburn try taking a teaspoon of apple cider vinegar followed by a glass of water.

10. Apple Cider Vinegar can help with allergies and stave off sinus infections.

Vinegar is also delicious in salad dressings!

And none of this is new. The well-known nursery rhyme about Jack and Jill going up that hill to fetch a pail of water dates back to at least the 18th century when Vinegar and brown paper were a home cure used to draw out bruises on the body.

Jack and Jill

Jack and Jill went up the hill
    To fetch a pail of water;
Jack fell down and broke his crown,
    And Jill came tumbling after.

Up Jack got, and home did trot,
    As fast as he could caper;
He went to bed and plastered his head
    With vinegar and brown paper.

Spiderman to the Rescue!

Ancient Greeks applied spiders' webs to cuts and
wounds. Apparently spiders coat their silk in
an antiseptic which can promote healing.

THE BOTTOM LINE

There's no easy way to say this, but we've all had that moment when we don't know which end to focus on first, only to find that they both erupt simultaneously.

Diarrhoea is wretched, and when it's accompanied by vomiting it can feel like your world is coming to an end. It probably isn't, but gastroenteritis is one of the most debilitating illnesses, both emotionally and physically.

Caused either by a virus, or by food poisoning, it can leave you dehydrated and in need of replacement body salts.

This is when your generously stocked store cupboard comes in handy.

Be sure to follow the instructions about how to use Rehydration sachets (Dioralyte etc) – the amount of water you need to dissolve them is scientifically worked out to give you the best results, so don't just guess.

The sachets will help replace salt, glucose and other essential electrolytes lost during dehydration.

In an emergency and if your store cupboard is a little bare, use a soft drink such as Coca Cola or Pepsi, Lucozade, Sprite, Ginger Ale or Lemonade diluted in a little water to reduce gassiness. Coconut water is another good source of hydration.

It's important not to eat for 24 hours after a bout of diarrhoea and vomiting – otherwise you will perpetuate the illness and slow your recovery.

Once you are feeling a little better – and 24 hours after the last episode of vomiting – you might like to introduce food in the form of the American BRAT diet.

- Bananas
- Rice
- Applesauce (or jam)
- Toast

The BRAT diet can help you recover from an upset stomach or diarrhoea by including "binding" foods. These are low-fibre foods that can help make your stools firmer.

Bananas, which are high in potassium, help replace nutrients your body has lost because of vomiting or diarrhoea.

This diet may also help ease the nausea and vomiting some women experience during pregnancy.

☞**DO** add other bland foods to the BRAT diet if you feel up to it. Savoury crackers, boiled potatoes or clear soups are recommended.

☞**DON'T** start eating dairy products and sugary or fatty foods until you are fully recovered. These foods may trigger nausea or lead to more diarrhoea.

∞∞∞∞∞∞∞∞∞∞∞∞∞∞∞ FOOD POISONING ∞∞∞∞∞∞∞∞∞∞∞∞∞∞∞

With all the same symptoms of gastroenteritis, food poisoning is one of the most dramatic and unpleasant ways to be ill. It can be quite dangerous, too. And it's largely avoidable.

If you are in any doubt about food hygiene, try this quiz:

All answers are either True or False

1. You can reheat leftovers as many times as you like.

2. If something is cooked on the outside it will definitely be cooked on the inside.

3. You should wash chicken and other poultry before cooking.

4. It is important to clean chopping boards/utensils after using them for raw meat.

5. You only need to wash your hands and clean kitchen surfaces when they look dirty.

6. Cooked rice can't be kept as long as other leftovers.

7. Food poisoning isn't serious, it just means an upset stomach.

8. Eating food after the 'use by' date won't hurt.

9. If it looks OK and smells OK, it's safe to eat.

10. Eating food after the 'best before' date won't hurt.

Answers on Pages 103-105

—————————— The Truth About Chicken Soup ——————————

Chicken soup is a well-known cure-all. Good for recovery, good for cheering you up, good for the soul, they say. And it turns out to be true!

Research in the American Journal of Therapeutics showed that Carnosine – a compound found in chicken soup – helped the body's immune system fight the early stages of flu.

Dr Stephen Rennard, of the University of Nebraska Medical Centre, Omaha, tested volunteers and was able to show that the soup inhibited the migration of infection-fighting cells in the body and helped reduce cold symptoms.

Vegetarians' do not despair!

What Dr Rennard couldn't do was identify the exact ingredients in the soup that made it effective against colds.

The soup he used contained chicken, onions, sweet potatoes, parsnips, turnips, carrots, celery stems, parsley, salt and pepper.

Researchers found other, non-chicken soups, had a similar effect, so worth investing in a good make of soup – or better still make your own.

Once you are back to normal – no matter the cause of your illness – it is important to start eating well as soon as you can.

Within 48 hours of dietary neglect the immune system becomes less effective at combatting disease.

HOSPITAL ETIQUETTE

There was a time when, if you had a bout of tonsillitis, you'd be under the surgeon's knife and eating a bowl of ice cream and jelly before you could say 'but I might need them later!'

Nowadays tonsillectomy is less common and you are more likely to be in hospital if you've got a broken bone or been in an accident.

If you are in for surgery to remove some bit of you, take comfort from the Top Five most useless body parts

- Tonsils
- Adenoids
- Gall Bladder
- Wisdom Teeth
- Appendix

(there are others, like your third eyelid or your sinuses, but they can't easily be removed).

So you can kiss goodbye to all of these without feeling too much sadness. You will feel drowsy after the operation. You may feel a bit sick. You will definitely have a sore throat and feel thirsty. You ought not to feel any real pain; your stitches might itch, it might hurt when you laugh, but that's all part of the recuperation process.

Your stay might be mercifully short, or not. In which case it's worth bearing in mind that (most) nurses are human beings too. They might have had a row with their partner, the dog might have thrown up in their favourite shoes, or they might just have failed their driving test for the umpteenth time. They ought still to be kind to you, but everyone has off days. Try asking them how *they* feel, for a change.

☞**DO** be co-operative. Don't pretend to be asleep when the nurses need to carry out some procedure – however unpleasant – they'll only come back later.

But don't suffer in silence – if you need pain relief ask for it. The same with food and drink, but don't be greedy. Ask your Recovery Team to bring you your favourite food and drink – having first checked that it's allowed.

☞**DON'T** argue about the fact that you can't have your preferred alcoholic beverage. And don't be one of those people who are seen standing in the doorway to the hospital, drip attached, sometimes in a wheelchair, having a cigarette. It's really not a good look. Use the opportunity of your confinement to quit. Or add nicotine patches to your shopping list if you really can't, having first checked that they aren't going to significantly worsen your condition.

If you're having physiotherapy in hospital be grateful for it. Once you are back at home it will be far harder to do the exercises without someone standing over you with a stick. So make the best use of the time.

Unless you are very poorly you will get bored quite quickly. And the wait until visiting hours will seem long. Try not to distract the nurses just because you want company. Learn Sudoku, do the crossword or organise your photographs.

Or you could try deciphering your hospital notes. That chart at the end of your bed with a variety of dots and squiggles. It might make very illuminating reading. Before patients had the right to see what doctors wrote about them – at the GP's surgery as well as in hospital – the quacks had some very interesting acronyms for their patients.

UBI:

Unexplained Beer Injury

GPO:

Good for Parts Only

TEETH:

Tried Everything Else, Try Homoeopathy

LOBNH:

Lights on But Nobody Home

FLK:

Funny Looking Kid

GLM:

Good Looking Mother

OAP:

Over-Anxious Parent

SIG:

Stroppy Ignorant Girl

TBP:

Total Bloody Pain

WAW:

What A Wally

If you see any of those you might want to modify your behaviour, or ask your Mum to dress up, or down, when she next visits.

—————————— Most Commonly Broken Bones ——————————

According to The Health and Social Care Information Centre, the most commonly broken bones in England in 2012-2013 were:

Femur (thigh bone)	113,057
Forearm	59,967
Lower leg (inc ankle)	58,987
Shoulder & upper arm	39,523
Skull & facial bones	30,302
Wrist & hand	29,994
Lumber spine & pelvis	28,777
Ribs & thoracic spine	14,195
Foot (except ankle)	8,767
Neck	5,014

Broken bones take time to heal and it's not something you can hurry.

You may be in a plaster cast or brace for anything from 3 – 6 weeks, depending on the severity of the break and which bone.

After the cast comes off you may have a further 3 weeks to 4 months of physiotherapy or other exercises to strengthen and rebuild muscles and restore mobility.

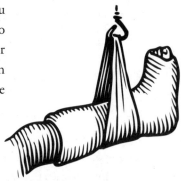

—————————Caring for Your Plaster Cast—————————

☞**DO** keep your arm or leg raised and resting on a pillow for the first few days to help the swelling go down.

☞**DON'T** get your plaster cast wet. This will weaken it and your bone won't be properly supported.

Buy a cast protector – some larger supermarkets with pharmacies stock them, or search **www.limboproducts.co.uk.** These products protect your cast from getting wet so you can have a bath in relative comfort and also allow you to go out when it's raining.

Failing that, use a plastic bag to cover up the cast when you have a bath or shower. Seal the bag with sticky tape or a rubber band to make it as water-tight as possible.

☞**DO** remove the bag as soon as you can after bathing, to avoid causing sweating, which could also damage the cast.

Or buy a cheap hose attachment to fit to your bath taps and instead of filling the bath, have a hand-held shower sitting or lying in the bath with your plastered leg resting on the side of the bath, out of the way of the water.

☞**DO** contact your hospital for advice as soon as possible if your cast does get wet.

☞**DO** resist the temptation to use a knitting needle, or indeed anything at all sharp, to relieve an itch in a plaster cast. This is a very bad idea indeed because if you break the skin you could develop an infection.

Mild hay-fever tablets might help reduce the itch, but ask first if they are suitable for you.

☞**DO** exercise any joints that aren't covered by the cast - such as your elbow, knee, fingers or toes – to help improve your circulation and prevent a frozen shoulder and stiff elbow joints.

☞**DON'T** walk with your leg in plaster – use crutches and keep the weight off.

─────────────── Plaster Cast Problems ───────────────

☞**DO get immediate medical attention:**

◦ If you ever see any blood seeping through or out of a plaster cast.
◦ If there is an unpleasant smell or discharge coming from your cast.
◦ If your plaster cast still feels too tight after keeping it elevated for 24 hours.
◦ If your fingers or toes on the affected limb feel swollen, tingly, painful (even after taking painkillers) or numb.
◦ If your fingers or toes turn blue or white.
◦ If your cast is broken or cracked.
◦ If the skin underneath or around the edge of your cast feels sore.

While you are in plaster and your muscles are not being used it's likely your limb will shrink. If your plaster cast starts to chaff you might want to put something between the cast and your skin to protect from rubbing.

A thin scarf or handkerchief might work or, in extremis, you could, like my younger brother John, try stuffing sanitary towels down your cast. But be prepared for strange looks as you hobble to the loo in the local pub, leaving a trail of them behind you.

If the cast becomes really loose do go to A&E or back to the Fracture Clinic.

──────────────Plaster Cast Management──────────────

To help minimise the misery of having a leg in plaster try some of these tips:

- Ask for an extra pair of crutches and leave one at the top of the stairs so you don't have to drag your only pair up and down the stairs all the time.

- Buy some rubber grips for the crutches – the supports might be quite sore on your hands after a while. Or improvise – bunion pads are good for creating a cushion to protect the bit between your thumb and fingers. Pipe lagging is another option.

- Ask about an **air boot**. These are sometimes offered for minor injuries instead of plaster casts. Some can be used without the need for crutches.

- When going up and down steps or stairs remember always to use your good leg first when you are going up, and your bad leg first when going down steps.

- NEVER sit down with crutches still on your arms, this is how you'll break your arms too! Always take your arms out, put the crutch handles together and sit down using your free hand to steady yourself.

- Be sure your crutches are the right height. When you stand up straight with your arms by your side the crutch handle should be a wrist level.

- If you're really struggling to get to the loo, and especially if going for a pee means climbing a flight of stairs, ask for a commode.

- Be especially careful not to fall – plaster casts are fragile and can easily break.

- Try eating plenty of good proteins and calcium.

- Reduce your intake of caffeine and alcohol as these can slow down the bone-knitting-together process and delay recovery.

There is some anecdotal evidence that eating strong fish oils keeps the skin from drying up and helps prevent itching inside the cast.

─────────── Preparing For a Day on Crutches ───────────

Until you've had a broken leg, or an arm in plaster, you won't know about the joys of trying to make a cup of tea and carry it back to your chair while on crutches.

Here's how to do it:
Assuming you are in the house and on your own, there are a few essentials for getting through the day.

First, get something to carry everything you need with you, for example:

- A large carrier bag with long handles which you can put round your neck like a nosebag
- An apron with deep pockets

- A Bumbag
- A Rucksack
- A Crutchbag

Items to put into the bag:
- Your mobile phone
- House keys
- A Thermos mug and/or a Thermos flask
- Packet of biscuits
- Plate & cutlery for mealtimes
- Tissues or a loo roll
- Wet wipes or hand sanitiser
- Any medication that you're taking
- Newspaper or TV guide
- Bottle of water.

You might be offered a perching stool by your Occupational Therapist, so you can sit on that while you make your flask of tea, sandwiches, fill up your water bottle or heat up some soup.

Despite all these aids to prevent you having to move around too much, don't forget to exercise as advised by your physio. Wriggle toes and fingers, stretch the limbs that aren't injured, do any chair exercises that will keep your circulation moving and maintain a bit of muscle tone.

Get into a routine if that helps, invite a friend round to exercise with you or, if you're watching TV, decide that during every ad break you'll do your wriggles and flexes and clenches.

A word of warning!
One thing that doesn't stop
when you break a bone is hair
growth. When the plaster
comes off it will take with it
all the hair on your leg or
arm. It will be painful and
you might even want to
take some Paracetamol or
Ibuprofen beforehand to
slightly reduce the pain.

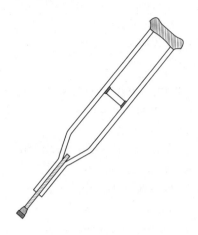

I enjoy convalescence. It is the part
that makes the illness worthwhile.

George Bernard Shaw

CONVALESCING IN STYLE

Wherever you decide to convalesce make sure there is as much natural light as possible. Keep curtains open for as long as there is daylight.

If the weather allows, and you have a garden, try to spend some time each day outside. If you can't, ask your Recovery Team to buy or lend you some house plants. Studies have shown that a bit of greenery and looking at nature can reduce stress and help create feelings of well-being.

Colour generally helps lift the spirits and especially during a prolonged period of convalescence. Surround yourself with anything brightly coloured – cushions, blankets, that luminous pink jumper or your bright blue tracky bottoms. If all else fails ask for flowers – it's one of the reasons people used to take flowers to patients in hospital, although that's discouraged nowadays.

Variety of form and brilliancy of colour
in the objects presented to patients
is the actual means of recovery

Florence Nightingale

Music is a great companion and comforter. Singing along will benefit your lungs and circulation as well as cheering you up.

You may still need plenty of sleep but it's important to sleep at night and stay awake, as far as possible, during the day.

Sleep expert Professor Colin Espie explains that the amount of sleep we need varies from person to person, and is different at different stages in life. The trick is to figure out how much sleep you need and then be sure to get it. There's no point in trying to force yourself to abide by the notion of one-size fits all and setting your alarm clock by the national average of 8 hours. Some people need more sleep and others less.

And it's the deep, restorative REM sleep that we need, not the light superficial stuff.

The professor says that sleep/wake needs are not taken into account enough when planning care and recuperation. "Good sleep and good wakefulness are every bit as central to a person's wellbeing as food and hydration."

As a convalescent try to be out in daylight as much as possible to maximise the positive effects of light on synchronising your biological clock.

Your Recovery Team will be invaluable during your convalescence. But manage them well. Unless you have just had your plaster cast removed this is not a time to crack open the champagne and stay up into the wee small hours.

This is a time for some company, but not a party; it's an opportunity to watch those DVDs that have been gathering dust, while your Recovery Team prepares cups of tea, jugs of juice and light snacks.

Humour is often called the best medicine, so if you can pick a classic comedy, or borrow one from a friend or even the local library, and have a good laugh, all the better.

If you've run out of DVDs or you want to do something that allows for more chat, don't disregard old-fashioned pastimes like cards and board games. They can be hugely satisfying without being too energetic.

GETTING BACK ON YOUR FEET

Once you're out of bed you need to get moving again. Too much time spent in bed can cause muscles to weaken, joints to seize up, feelings of fatigue and general inertia.

Exercise – done gradually and gently – is essential to recovery and to well-being.

In fact, if exercise could be written as a prescription it would be prescribed for:

- Strengthening joints and bones
- Improving muscle condition
- Improving co-ordination and balance
- Lowering harmful cholesterol
- Tackling depression and improving mood
- Reducing blood pressure
- Reducing the risk of diabetes
- Reducing the risk of heart attack and stroke

Ask one of your Recovery Team to accompany you on short walks, even if only to the shops to begin with. Gradually build up to full strength and then, just because you've gone back to work/college don't give up on the exercise. It also improves the functioning of the immune system, helps reduce the risk of developing some cancers, and altogether lengthens life.

Buy yourself a pedometer or download an app that monitors how far you have walked and your heart rate. Anything to keep you interested in exercising.

If you are recovering from a broken bone you will have been given specific exercises to rebuild your strength. Be sure to do what's recommended and enlist the help of the fiercest member of your Recovery Team to stand over you with a Big Stick if necessary.

Simple daily mobility exercises:

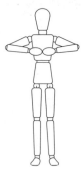 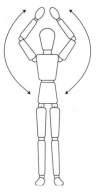 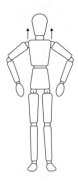

Arms to chest and out x 10   Arms up and down x 10   Shoulders up and down x 5

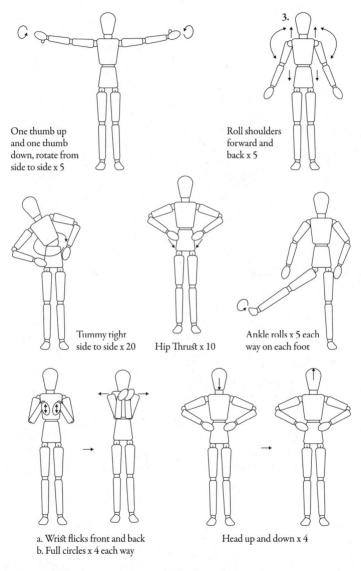

One thumb up and one thumb down, rotate from side to side x 5

Roll shoulders forward and back x 5

Tummy right side to side x 20

Hip Thrust x 10

Ankle rolls x 5 each way on each foot

a. Wrist flicks front and back
b. Full circles x 4 each way

Head up and down x 4

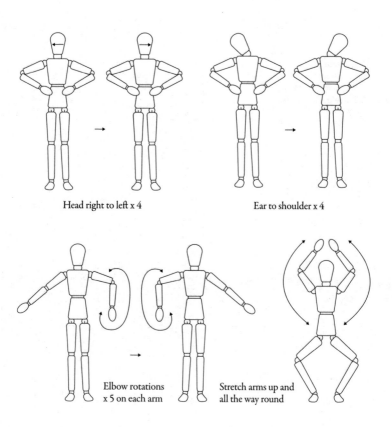

Head right to left x 4

Ear to shoulder x 4

Elbow rotations
x 5 on each arm

Stretch arms up and
all the way round

According to the World Health Organisation
40% of ill health in the developed
world is caused by poor diet.

KEEPING WELL

We all know the long list of things that are bad for us; smoking, too much alcohol, sugar, fat, caffeine, red meat and so on.

So what's good for you? Well, if you want to give your immune system a boost, especially after an illness, but also maintain good health, these are some foods that ought to be in your diet.

Lean meat, poultry, eggs, legumes (that's beans, lentils, peas, soya-beans), nuts and seeds (**for Protein**).

Oranges, lemons and grapefruit (**a good source of Bioflavonoids**).

Broccoli, citrus fruits and onions (**for Quercetin** – which has anti-oxidant, anti-histamine and anti-inflammatory properties).

Eggs, seeds, nuts and whole grain cereals (**provides Zinc** – essential for healthy development and good for boosting the immune system).

Watermelon, kale, Brussels sprouts, spinach and cabbage (**Glutathione** – necessary for many bodily processes, including tissue building and repair, making chemicals and proteins, and for the immune system).

Other so called super-foods, known to be beneficial to health, include sweet potatoes, blueberries, garlic, green tea, cherry juice, wild salmon, butternut squash, tropical fruits, red and sweet peppers.

If you're feeling a bit run down try a tonic, rather than another coffee or a can of something fizzy. You can buy tonics in supermarkets, chemists and health food shops.

Get plenty of sleep, take regular exercise and fill your lungs with fresh air.

~~~~~~~~~~~~~~~~~~~~~~~~~~~~~~~~~~ MEDICAL MYTHS ~~~~~~~~~~~~~~~~~~~~~~~~~~~~~~~~~~
catching cold

How often have you heard : "You'll catch your death if you don't wrap up." Or "Don't leave the house with wet hair".

In fact, you can't catch a cold by being cold. Colds are caused by viruses (over 200 different varieties), so in order to catch one you have to be infected by a germ. This can happen when you inhale air containing an infected person's sneeze or cough. You can also get a cold virus by shaking hands with an infected person or by using something where the virus has settled. This might be a door handle, a bannister rail or a phone.

66 STARVE A FEVER, FEED A COLD 99

This well-known saying is often dismissed as an old wives' tale, but eating does stimulate the immune response that will work to kill a cold virus, so it makes sense to eat when you have a cold.

If you can't face food, it won't matter if you miss a couple of meals as long as you are drinking plenty of fluids. Just don't deliberately starve yourself (unless you have gastroenteritis).

" FLU VACCINATIONS CAN MAKE YOU ILL "

When you get a Flu jab you are, in fact, getting the bit of the virus that stimulates your body to create antibodies. That way you're ready to kill off the flu virus if you come into contact with it. The bit of the vaccine that might actually give you flu has been switched off. The only reason to avoid some vaccines is if you have a severe allergy to eggs, because eggs are used to create the vaccines.

No vaccine is 100-percent effective, so there is still a chance you can get the flu after receiving the jab, but that doesn't mean the vaccination gave it to you.

" COFFEE CAN SOBER YOU UP "

If you've had too much to drink, no amount of coffee is going to sober you up. The only thing that will do that is time.

The liver processes about one standard drink per hour. That's to say - a bottle of beer, a small glass of wine or a small glass of spirits - so if you're drinking more than that every 60 minutes, you'll have alcohol in your system — and be suffering the effects — for as long as it takes for the liver to do its work. Because coffee is a stimulant it can counteract the sedative effect of alcohol, but it won't sober you up.

The best way to minimise the effects of a hangover is to eat before you drink, to drink a glass of water between each alcoholic drink, not to mix different types of alcohol and not to drink to excess. Simples!

———————————— About Alcohol ————————————

Alcohol is a diuretic – it removes fluids from the body and can cause extreme dehydration. Symptoms of dehydration include headaches, sickness, upset stomach, disturbed sleep, dizziness. These are the symptoms of a classic hangover.

To minimise the effects of a hangover:

◦ Don't drink on an empty stomach. Carbohydrates such as pasta or rice will help slow down the body's absorption of alcohol.

◦ Drink water or non-fizzy soft drinks between each alcoholic drink. Fizzy drinks aren't as useful because they speed up the absorption of alcohol into your system.

◦ Find the drink that suits you best – some people do better with wine than spirits. For others it's the exact opposite.

◦ Drink a pint of water before you go to sleep and continue to take sips of water throughout the night whenever you wake up.

———————————— The Morning After ————————————

Everyone has their own favourite recovery routine after a night on the tiles. A fry-up breakfast, Irn Bru or Coca Cola, Vegemite, hot food, cold food, isotonic sports drinks, vitamin C. The important things are to rehydrate and not put any additional strain on your body while it sorts itself out.

◦ Replace lost fluids by drinking bland liquids that are easy on the digestive system – water, freshly squeezed juices or smoothies which will help replace lost vitamins and minerals.

◦ Painkillers can help with headaches and muscle cramps.

Take Paracetamol rather than aspirin which may irritate the stomach and make the nausea and sickness worse. But be aware that painkillers will put an extra strain on your liver and may slow up the recovery process, even if they do relieve the pain.

- An antacid might help to settle your stomach.

- Sugary foods and drinks may give you a temporary lift and make you feel less wobbly.

- Eat bland foods that are easy to digest - soup, plain savoury crackers, yoghurt, toast.

- Drinking more alcohol ('hair of the dog') will only delay the inevitable and is therefore not recommended.

- If you've had a lot to drink it's best to avoid alcohol altogether for 48 hours to give your system the best chance of recovery.

———————— Most Frequent Illness Searches ————————

According to **www.patient.co.uk** these were the things that people most commonly searched for in 2013:

1. Shingles

About 1 in 5 people have shingles at some time in their life. It occurs because the chickenpox virus which has been lying dormant in your body has been reactivated. A vaccine against shingles for older people was introduced in 2013.

2. Chickenpox

Most children have chickenpox at some stage, and full recovery is usual.

3. Swollen glands

If you are fighting an infection, the lymph glands nearby swell quickly and become tender. This is usually your immune system 'fighting off' infecting germs.

4 . Acid reflux

About 1 adult in 3 has some heartburn every few days and nearly 1 adult in 10 has heartburn at least once a day.

5. Hypothyroidism

This condition causes a slowing of the body's functions. The symptoms develop gradually. About 1 in 50 women, and about 1 in 1,000 men develop hypothyroidism at some time in their life.

6. Leg cramps

Many people have an occasional leg cramp. However, they can occur frequently in some people and are more common in older people.

7. Liver function tests

Whilst not a condition, liver function tests featured highly on the list. Liver function tests can help diagnose and monitor liver disorders for this most hard-working of organs.

8. Rectal bleeding

There are many causes of rectal bleeding. The most common type of rectal bleeding is mild.

9. Piles

About half the people in the UK develop one or more haemorrhoids at some stage.

10. Knee injury

In at number 10, knee ligament injury. Usually from a direct blow to the knee, from sport, or a fall.

THE WORLD'S SICKEST PLACES

According to the Global Burden of Disease Study 2010, these are the illest countries in the world.

Unhealthiest countries

Men	Women
1. Burkina Faso	1. Liberia
2. Chad	2. Burundi
3. Democratic Republic of Congo	3. Afghanistan
4. Malawi	4. Malawi
5. Zimbabwe	5. Zimbabwe
6. Mozambique	6. Mozambique
7. Swaziland	7. Swaziland
8. Central African Republic	8. Lesotho
9. Lesotho	9. Central African Republic
10. Haiti	10. Haiti

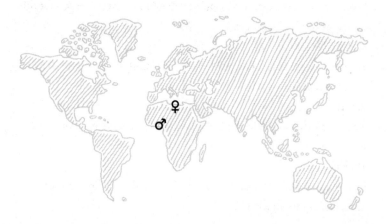

───────── **Healthiest countries** ─────────

Men	Women
1. Japan	1. Japan
2. Singapore	2. South Korea
3. Switzerland	3. Spain
4. Spain	4. Singapore
5. Italy	5. Taiwan
6. Australia	6. Switzerland
7. Canada	7. Andorra
8. Andorra	8. Italy
9. Israel	9. Australia
10. South Korea	10. France

DATES FOR YOUR DIARY

Toothache Day
9th February

•

Sexual and Reproductive Health Awareness Day
12th February

•

Purple Day for Epilepsy
26th March

•

National Doctor's Day
30th March

•

Autism Awareness Day
2nd April

•

World No Tobacco Day
31st May

•

Virus Appreciation Day
3rd October

•

World Mental Health Day
10th October

•

Global Handwashing Day
15th October

•

World AIDS Day
1st December

—————— A Song That Could Help Save Your Life ——————

The first rule of keeping well is hygiene. Hand washing is an art, not something to be done in a hurry or be overlooked, especially in a public place. The ideal time spent washing your hands after you've been to the loo is the time it takes to sing "Happy Birthday" twice through.

Try it now. Out loud, or in your head, depending on where you are. Pick someone whose birthday is sometime around now, or make up a name. Or serenade yourself.

Off you go!

And again. With gusto.

And now your hands should be properly clean.

The Proper Way to Wash Your Hands

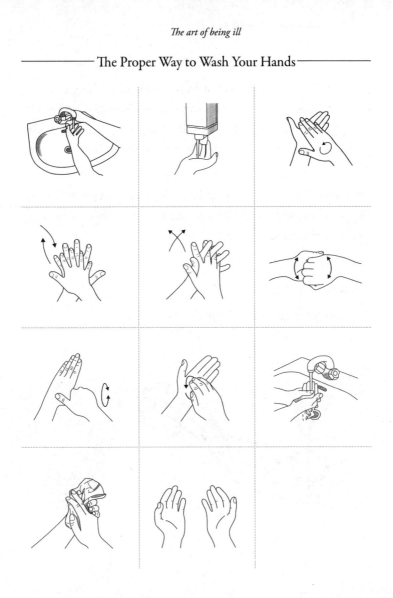

——— And If You Don't Wash Your Hands ———
Source: Public Health England

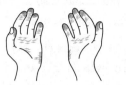

After using toilet

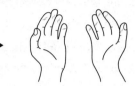

Washed, after using toilet

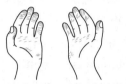

After handling raw meat

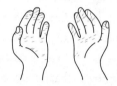

Washed, after handling raw meat

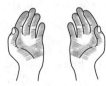

After handling old dishcloth

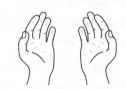

Washed, after handling old dishcloth

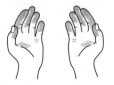

After handling raw chicken

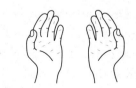

Washed, after handling raw chicken

ANSWERS TO THE FOOD QUIZ

1. You can reheat leftovers as many times as you like.

False ∘ you should only reheat leftovers once. The more times you cool and reheat a food, the more potential there is for food poisoning – bacteria might grow and multiply because the food is cooled too slowly. Also make sure the food is reheated thoroughly, so that it is steaming hot all the way through.

2. If something is cooked on the outside it will definitely be cooked on the inside.

False ∘ most forms of cooking involve heat penetrating the food from the outside, so although the surface may be cooked the centre may not be. It is therefore important to make sure that the food is thoroughly cooked all the way through.

3. You should wash chicken and other poultry before cooking.

False ∘ research has shown that bacteria in water droplets can spread easily, by splashing onto worktops, dishes and other foods. This makes food poisoning more likely to occur.

4. It is important to clean chopping boards/utensils after using them for raw meat.

True ∘ bacteria can transfer from the meat to the chopping boards/utensils. If they are then used for ready-to-eat foods without being washed, that bacteria can then transfer to food. This is known as cross-contamination.

5. You only need to wash your hands and clean kitchen surfaces when they look dirty.

False ∘ you can't see bacteria with the naked eye, so there is no way to tell if your hands and work surfaces are clean. You should therefore always wash your hands and surfaces before and after food preparation. Evidence has also shown that bacteria spread more readily in the presence of moisture, so always DRY YOUR HANDS after washing them thoroughly.

6. Cooked rice can't be kept as long as other leftovers.

True ∘ Leftover cooked rice is fine to eat as long as it gets cooled and refrigerated quickly after cooking and eaten within 24 hours. This is because rice can contain a particularly tough type of bacteria that can survive heating. Most other leftovers are safe to eat up to two days after cooking. See Q1 re reheating of leftovers.

7. Food poisoning isn't serious, it just means an upset stomach.

False ∘ Although most cases of food poisoning are mild and last only a day or two, some can be far more serious, even deadly. This is rare, but it is good to remember the simple 4 Cs for good food hygiene; cleaning, cooking, chilling and avoiding cross-contamination.

8. Eating food after the 'use by' date won't hurt.

False ∘ A 'use by' date tells you how long food will stay **safe** and is put on food that 'goes off' quickly. The dates are worked out by scientific testing. Don't be tempted to eat food after the 'use by' date on the label, even if it looks and smells fine. NB – do not confuse this with 'best before' dates which are about food quality not safety.

9. If it looks OK and smells OK, it's safe to eat.

False ◦ Although a bad smell or taste are signs that food has 'gone off', these signs often aren't caused by germs that give you food poisoning. So the food's appearance, smell or taste aren't reliable warning signs. Instead, stick to the 'use by' date and storage instructions on the packet.

10. Eating food after the 'best before' date won't hurt.

True ◦ 'Best before' dates are about food quality not safety. They are usually found on foods which last a long time. If food has passed its 'best before' date it doesn't mean it's unsafe, but it might have started to lose its colour, flavour or texture.

Courtesy of Food Standards Agency January 2014 – Food safety – what do you know?

─────────────── Summing up ───────────────

No-one really enjoys being ill, but we're not invincible and most of us will be ill at some time or other. Maybe just for a few days, or maybe for longer.

Someone once said that 'death is Nature's way of telling you to slow down'. But by then it's a bit late! I'd say illness is Nature's way of telling you to slow down. And it's worth taking notice and giving your body the best chance of a quick recovery. You have nothing to lose and everything to gain.

Keep well!

Be careful about reading health books.
You may die of a misprint.

Mark Twain

———————————— Thanks to ————————————

The Sinclair family, Willa King, Pollokshields Library, Catherine Prentice, Dr. Sarah Jarvis and **www.patient.co.uk**, Zoë Strachan, Graham Jones, Elizabeth Goodall, Jonathan Atkinson, Mrs Lorna Searle, Amanda Cooksley, Adrian Searle, Robbie Guillory, Kouki Gharra and Adam Turner.

——————— About the author ———————

Jill Sinclair is a television programme maker, DVD producer and writer. She has written articles, reviews and profiles for the Guardian, Telegraph, Glasgow Herald and London Evening Standard, as well as numerous magazines. She is the writer of a blog about moving back home to look after her demented dad and is working on her first novel.